A Kind of Mercy

poems by

Sharon A Foley

Finishing Line Press
Georgetown, Kentucky

A Kind of Mercy

Copyright © 2025 by Sharon A Foley
ISBN 979-8-89990-189-8 First Edition
All rights reserved under International and Pan-American Copyright Conventions. No part of this book may be reproduced in any manner whatsoever without written permission from the publisher, except in the case of brief quotations embodied in critical articles and reviews.

ACKNOWLEDGMENTS

Thanks to the literary magazines who first published my poems, some under different titles:

Solstice: A Magazine of Diverse Voices, Fall/Winter 2012: I Think I Might Join the Convent
South Florida Poetry Journal, November 2016: 36 Girls, Lights Out, No Talking
Speckled Trout Review, Fall 2022: My Best Friend Leaves the Convent
Euphony, Spring 2023: Year Four, I'm Chief of the Laundry
SWWIM, December 13, 2023: A Visit to My Bedridden Father

Publisher: Leah Huete de Maines
Editor: Christen Kincaid
Cover Art: Grey Held
Author Photo: Heller Photography
Cover Design: Elizabeth Maines McCleavy

Order online: www.finishinglinepress.com
   also available on amazon.com

Author inquiries and mail orders:
Finishing Line Press
PO Box 1626
Georgetown, Kentucky 40324
USA

Contents

I Think I Might Join the Convent 1
Day Fourteen as a Postulant 2
Softball on the Hill 3
36 Girls Lights Out, No Talking 4
My Best Friend Leaves the Convent 5
April Fools at the Novitiate 6
Thank God They Changed to a New Habit 7
Year Four, I'm Chief of the Laundry 8
Once a Month Meditation on Death 9
Christmas Pageant in the Convent 10
Second Thoughts After My First Vows 11
A Visit to My Bedridden Father 12
What Holds Me Now 13
Sister Marilyn, Our Beloved Belizean 14
Summer in the Convent Kitchen 15
The First Time I See My Confessor's Face 16
Matriculation at Salve Regina College 17
Student Teacher at St. Mary's Academy 18
Sister Agnes and Father Charles Break Their Vows 20
Custom Made for My Final Vow 21
From the Convent to a Red Bungalow 22
The Truth about Social Justice 23
Abandoned in the Inner City 24
My Accusation Knocking on Her Door 25
I've Got Leaving on My Mind 26
A Kink in the Road 27
Revelation on the Roundabout 28
My Final Night as a Nun 29
Exchanging My Vows for a Car 30

Listen and you will live
Isaiah 55:3

I Think I Might Join the Convent

Sister Frederick sponsors me.
I am the first one,
the feather in her barren cap.

I sneak out of personal
typing class for the booty
of her time, and because I'm bored.

I love her foyer, her vestibule,
I love her rapture.

Steel grey eyes pierce me
though she keeps her face calm.
I love her kinetic mind.

Once I saw her dancing
with her father. We drank the Brandy Alexanders.
I love the fondness in her voice.

Her life is velvet:
black veil, white scapular over
her breast.

What is it about her
that ignites my thirst?

Day Fourteen as a Postulant

Stony cold in the light flooded chapel, I sit
as the mistress holds a hinged wooden instrument
called a clapper, tapping the wood together
to make a sound reverberate. I lift

myself, stand, and clasp my hands under
my cape, elbows out like bird wings,
shoulders drooped, head up. I still have not
yet mastered the evenflow of breath.

Holy candles illumine the stark darkness
I am here like a lamb, unknowing.

I face Sister Fran and chant,
"You are beautiful" though I do not know
what beauty means in this convent,
I do know we sing of beauty.

Softball on the Hill

I would like to be benched for the season
but I step up to bat.
In this diamond tender mercy begins.
I pin back the cape of my postulant dress.
Sister Ellen yells, *Take the lead out*
and she coaches me how to swing.
When up to bat, I make a sacrifice bunt,
run to first and find a strange angel there.
When it's our turn in the outfield
there are no mitts. Their fouls are
redeemed by the softball God.
When the batter swings,
fear is my curve.

36 Girls, Lights Out, No Talking

We are Sisters masked in pantomime
who shut our lips after the night toll.
Our undergarments dwell in meshed bags,
stacked in the basket on the bathroom floor
ready to be placed in the front loaders
at dawn. All of this I can bear.

As for the bras—we must wash them
ourselves, like cleansing our souls
of dinginess
                          I wash my bra
six basins in a straight row, all of us washing
and six plastic bags
where each bra in its solitude welcomes
what tiny organisms might thrive the night.

While we are asleep, the Angel Raphael dispels
any thoughts of singularity. The common
wash is hung to dry, by some other angel
                          in the gated yard. Day's end,
it's all returned—the dingy whites,
                my striking pink bra
                I swear to cherish.

My Best Friend Leaves the Convent

Still I wonder: homesick or frailty?
Hard to follow the rigor of solitude?
I never had visions of her with boys
but maybe?

The note at the top of the stairs
just said *Sister Mary went home today.*

I wanted to ask her why she left
but I am entrenched with nuns.
Nothing more should be asked.
Nothing more would be said.

On my descent to the chapel, I look
down at my black clunky shoes. Each step
makes a squeak on the polished stair.
Chrysanthemums embolden the altar.

I fix my eyes on Sister Mary Lomax,
the organist who plays like Bach.
The chamber swells. Something
leaps in me: a shooting star contained.

April Fools at the Novitiate

Sister Peter Marie who has baked bread
in the silence of the altar bread room
keeping custody of her eyes
so as not to contaminate her mind
by reading newspapers
spread like linen on the tables

enters the dining room where she has set
the table not in the usual way but
special on this occasion for Sister Superior:
a huge metal mixing bowl, two feet in diameter,
flanked with a fork as long as my arms,
a butcher knife from the cook's kitchen,
and a wooden spoon that extended half way down the table.
I sit in silence to the right of Sister Superior
my nervousness reflected in the polished bowl.

We begin, *Bless us, O Lord,*
I dare not laugh. As the platters of food
move down the table, I can hardly
steady my hand to serve myself two pieces of fried baloney
and beans onto my plate. I pass
the platters to Sister Superior
who glares at Sister Peter Marie
as if she were a serial sinner.

Thank God They Changed to a New Habit

No need to shave my head before vesting
in the black garment head to toe,
nor to fret when I can't thread a needle
in the sewing room where
Sister Mary Baptist plans to teach
me how to make my own habit.

No, that's the way it used to be,
but the windows are open now.

Sister Ida gathers all of us postulants
in this most unusual fashion show.
For the first time we see
her wavy brown hair, her ankles and neck.
She is as brave as Coco Chanel.

The new habit is factory made
with a real silk collar, brilliant white.
The blue skirt is short—
It wouldn't stoop to touch the rain.
The black veil itself, only a wisp.

I am saved.

Fourth Year: I Am Chief of the Laundry

Bras, panties, shirts, the name of the sister
stitched on each piece.
There are also communal sheets

ready to be placed in the front loaders.
I'm the Angel Raphael who
hangs them out to dry in the gated yard.

No distractions, just chores.
I thank God for giving me
enough clothespins.

Rainy days I use heaters and pray
that the laundry will dry. Steam hits my face
as I throw a sheet over the metal bar.

I mangle smooth Mother Superior's sheets.
For all the others, I just fold them tight
and square, but leave a few

wrinkles in for Sister Mary Rosary
who at breakfast always takes
the last Sunday Bun.

Through this simple work
I consecrate the day.

Once a Month Meditation on Death

I am instructed by Mother Superior
to picture myself in a pine coffin.

I can feel myself clammy cold
but resist words from my meditation

book that worms are eating
through me. Still I pray

for the miracle that life is
forever. My father is dying.

I used to dream of having six children.
I exchange them to be in the common fold.

Here, where the light from the stained glass
falls, I am running

from my father's impending death
crazy for the dispassionate.

Christmas Pageant in the Convent

We are proud and poised
as stars of this pageant
standing in the nave
of this chapel like candles
waiting to be illuminated.

I stand in a gracious pose,
holding the wooden back of the pew
the way I held the barre
as a child in my first ballet class.
This past week I've rehearsed
my movement: swing my arms
out and up in a wide circle
end with humble folded hands.

Like all the others, I've been taught
to keep custody of our eyes
so I don't look at my Sisters as I dance.

Sister Monica sings in high soprano:
When Love was born
in the early morning hours…
I ready myself for my line:

Peace the message of Christmas

Second Thoughts After My First Vows

Silent as winter woods I pause
like a rest in a Bach chorale

to ask myself questions:
Why am I here?

*What does it mean
that my heart is for Mercy?*

I had to ask my parents
for gifts of a broom, and mop for Christmas

I did so willingly, though they
protested, dressed them up in red felt,

a six foot tall stocking
my name embroidered boldly.

Where does my heart rest?
I rest in God,

and what of the young priest who brought strawberries
in winter to the convent party?

How we sat by the fireplace
how I wanted him to stay.

A Visit with My Bedridden Father

It took two years to get permission
to see my father. I begin to imagine
my first words with him. *Beautiful day*

and he will answer, *Did you see the light
ripple on the stone wall?* But it rains
on my first visit. I say, *I wish the rain*

would stop. And he replies,
It always has. He's wearing a blue johnny
my mother made from one of his old shirts.

There is a cross above his bed,
a big wooden one with metal Jesus,
a touch of red paint on the wounds.

Dad's been carving oak into a bowl
he has rubbed with linseed oil.

My habit does not scrape his floor.
My breasts are bridled by a blue gamp.
I am Sister Mary Sharon now.

It's against the rules but for him
I lift my veil to show
wisps of my hair.

I have come from the high-ceilinged cloister.
In this tiny room
he seems so small to me.

What Holds Me Now

im of my father, William F. Foley
11/25/1906 to 12/24/1968

Loss keeps me tethered here
to you to belief

what I have is only now
to trust to attach,

the idea that on the other side
of loss is gain, the inward calming

like when the sea calms
to the waning moon

and forgets the crashing waves
I set my eyes on the horizon

a twin engine sailfish, adrift.

Sister Marilyn, Our Beloved Belizean

On Valentine's Day she joins the frolic
of the ranks, placing a decoration
from a cupcake in her crinoline cap.

I love hearing her regal tones when she
announces *Belize is a British Colony*
and when she notes the beauty of the cayes
the way I revere Cape Cod.

She quotes Wordsworth calling
us *a host of daffodils*
as we ascend the hill for play.

In Belize, she was a principal, but
here she just reminisces with her peers
about St. Catherine's. They speak in Creole.
Once I heard them joking about the incense
of refried beans, and genuflecting to
mangoes and cooked plantains.

After supper, she parades down the chapel aisle
the red accent bobbing above
the frizz of her hair and black crown

bowing to all of us
as if she were the queen
dancing with daffodils.

Summer in the Convent Kitchen

I watch Sister Bernadette, eyelashes curled,
her blue-opal eyes, and I see
the way Brother Martin melts

into easy conversation with her.
Like a kid sister, I'd watch her
getting ready for him

close to the mirror, the curling
gadget pressed two minutes,
then a hint of mascara.

They went blueberry picking.
I'm not sure where, but they've returned
and made our jam with orange zest.

Now, together, they plump raisins,
soak them in water in the cast iron pot
on the convent stove to soften

so careful. He drains the hot
liquid, holding the heavy pan
over the sink. She settles the fruit

on a kitchen towel. Her head bent down,
her hands stretched in blessing the dough
she kneads, but the mixture sticks.

He reaches for the linen
to clean each fingertip,
so tenderly as if they were

husband and wife. What is this
I'm feeling?
Is it jealousy?

The First Time I See My Confessor's Face

I knew his voice behind the screen
but had not expected him to be
so muscled, though covered with Graymour robes,
and his feet in sandals
like all the other Friars of the Atonement.

I don't remember what I had told him
in confession, but he must have sensed
my longing for men.
According to the language of the church,
I am "professed" now.
He's come to invite
Sister Kathy and I out to dinner.

I speak so soft
even my name.
The palms of his hands are smooth.

I don't know how the subject comes up
but we talk about love,
how hard it might be not to
fall in love.
He tells us, *I'm in love
with God.*

I don't know what came over me
but sitting in the booth,
I drape my arm
over his shoulder.
He touches the hem of
my light blue polyester dress.
I feel his hand on my knee.

Matriculation at Salve Regina College

I study *Romeo and Juliet*
on scholarship
as a Sister of Mercy,

and I can linger in my single room:
bed, desk, my own sink
and gaze out toward the ocean.

I walk the highest angriest cliffs
and know every step between
the convent and the highway.

On the inclines the eternal questions:
What keeps me at the convent?
Will I ever have children in my life?

Is there rebirth after death?
Why do my mashed potatoes flop
even though I call home for the recipe?

And why don't they let me drive?
Sister Constance, so huffy, gets to drive.
I don't understand why.

Nights we young sisters raid
the walk-in freezer for chocolate ice cream
or smoke Marlboros in Sister Margaret's room.

Our laughter breaks the cloister.
I do not pray to sleep
but rise to my own alarm.

Student Teaching at St. Mary's Academy

I love each child
in my open classroom
rock to their rhythm

and waltz to the
nuance of their steps.
I imagine each child

a gem to polish.
Sister Rose
instructs me

to hold tight the rein
on the Glancy girl,
keep the sensitive blond Mary Beth Healy in line,

in the tradition of
Sisters of Mercy, form them
to the shape we want.

I don't want to shape them.
I want them to bloom
into their own hues.

Sweet, little Lisa Briganti
dips her elbows in finger-paint
to draw a halo of her braided hair.

Ellen Murphy, the doctor's child,
always sits erect in the curve
of the small wooden chair.

Erin takes a book
wherever she goes
even to the lavatory,

and Tara, the shy girl,
Oh my gosh, how bright she is.
She's the one to watch.

Sister Agnes and Father Charles Break Their Vows

I'm not sure why she chooses to confide in
me, perhaps because I pretend to be
open as a Georgia O'Keefe flower,
but after mass she reveals
how she sneaks into the priest's quarters
to "cuddle" with him on his couch.
I imagine her with him melting
into the rich brown velvet herringbone,
and resting on ruby red pillows.
I pulse with energy as she speaks.

She asks me to be an angel
of protection for their love:
Stand watchful at our door.

I listen to her as a child listens,
in awe.
I know this hunger
also as my own.

Custom-Made For My Final Vows

On the altar, I wear the white dress,
my mother had custom-made for me,
by her seamstress. The mock Roman collar
gives it the look of a habit.
The small Mercy cross on my breast,
my brunette hair cut short in the new fashion.
I feel like a bride, the focus of everything.
The church is filled with family, friends,
and songs just for me. I feel the glow.
My blue eyes glance back—
though suddenly I feel the scratch
of polyester on my knees.

Father Paul wears as usual the white flowing chasuble,
the tapestry stole, and Jesus sandals,
his hair long and curly, like John Denver.

I tremble as I proclaim before the congregation
"I will be poor, I will obey, I will be chaste."
At the altar, I sign my vows on the dotted line.
Father Paul blesses the ring in his palms.
I take it and place the ring on my finger.

So I build a little shanty in my mind.
I am officially a nun.

From the Convent to a Red Bungalow

Six of us form a cozy type of Mercy.
New church rules allow us to move
from the brick convent that housed eighty
to a red bungalow we rent.
It's Sister Elena's turn to cook.

After we say grace, Sister Kathy
bursts into conversation. She vents and
compares our nation's revolution
with our moving out: freedom to bond
together rather than be herded, the right
to wear street clothes, not the blue habit.

Our artist, Sister Maria, tells with fervor
how she scavenges disparate threads:
marsh grass, strands of black sea weed,
commercial ribbon, and tinsel from our Christmas tree
to weave a blanket on a second-hand loom.

But Sister Maureen is the one who
weaves us all together. She talks about God
not the God above, but the One within.

After supper we walk the beach,
then sit in the living room shaking sand
from our toes. We massage one another's

feet, our fingers the pumice that
softens callousness.

The Truth about Social Justice

I follow the direction of Sister Ann,
but if you want to know the truth,
I don't really care about Cesar Chavez,
his boycott on lettuce, nor do I want
to carry the placard in a picket line
with my Sisters, though I do.

I make signs to protest the war
but decide not to go to the Federal Building
five o'clock, every Friday as my Sisters do.

I admire Sister Mary, who lectures me:
Don't teach our girls fairy tales.
Girls are strong. They don't need
men to rescue them.
I agree. The more I'm here
the more I realize that's true.

I listen and pray to be steadfast.

Abandoned in the Inner City

I thought we would sit all day
in this safe room: read, pray
and bask in the divine presence.
I want to feel the steadiness
of our retreat master we so love
and have nick-named Father Hans.

Instead he drives us to the inner city,
drops us off, one by one, alone,
stripped of pocketbooks, no ID,
only a sweater on our backs.
One sister is dropped near the homeless shelter,
another dropped at a convenience store.
I landed in front of St. Michael's Church.
No map to guide me, my mind
swirls with fear of riots and shootings,
the unfamiliar, but I trust
he will return.

I get out of the car and walk
the concrete sidewalks, cracked,
weeds popping through.
The ground is dry but there are patches
of green grass in front of
a few well-cared-for homes.
I meander the streets. Cars pass
but I meet no one. No stores,
no gas stations open. No
sound of fights or booms of guns
just the booming sound
of my own internal fretting.

My Accusation Knocking on Her Door

At a house meeting, she accuses me:
You are a manipulator,
her tone surged with judgment.

She is a tornado that tears me down
making me brittle
down to my bones. I rage.

I don't know how to feel my anger.
No one taught me—not at home, not here.
That stifled anger has been wrapped in a box,

but I want to break the ribbon now.
My plan is to knock on her door
until she answers, but as I come

closer, I run with my mind:
what will she say,
what will she do?

I stand there like this, every minute long.
I decide to let the coolness of the moon in.
The limbs of my body go limp

until there is no more intent
to storm. Only then can I knock
on her door and when she doesn't answer

I just keep knocking.

I've Got Leaving on My Mind

What makes a person whole?
In this brick convent, I dine with older
Sisters, but I don't belong here anymore.

A daylily who limps toward the end
of summer, I study so I can heal.
As I wonder what kind of person

I am, a gap forms in me,
sometimes a gouging loneliness.
I've given up on the long list

of friends busy now
with husbands
and children.

I've lived in communities of eight and twelve Sisters
smothered by their rules—the glasses go to the right
of the sink, not the left that feels better to me.

Life is the slow rise of sun through fog
a vision refracted.
I'm ready for a swerve in the road.

A Kink in the Road

I'm leaving the convent, decision done,
the defined path I've lived three decades
over. Restlessness gushes open

like a river mouth into ocean
leaving home when
home is already gone.

Sister Maureen and I take a walk
through a field, bordered by marsh grass
Irish feet treading softly on grounds

more sacred than a convent cloister.
She is the first person I tell.
We are tales of Mercy, drinking holy wine

Revelation on the Roundabout

I lose my way in the center
of these pathless woods.
Every stretch of my limbs

reaching out to God. Clouds
shaped like lions spread
across the horizon. Day lingers.

Lord, how will you guide me
toward the first indwelling?
You have brought me

to this empty playground:
swing sets, slides, jungle gym.
I climb onto the broken down

roundabout, splintered wood
touching my thighs.
You spin me and distract me from pain.

I contemplate
beauty infused—
earth's most mystical spin.

My Final Night as a Nun

I kneel on the carpeted floor, and hold
on to the quilted spread. Holy Mary,
Virgin Mother of God, keep me safe.
I will bring you white carnations,
the sweetest incense and chant your name.

Protect me from lightning strikes, robbers,
and heresies that threaten my belief
that the sun spins each day for you.

O lady up there, give me a sign,
a mallard in my vernal pond,
the long-heralded heron landing on my roof

Exchanging My Vows for a Car

They sold me a car and sent me forth with
a bachelor's and two Masters Degrees,
a trade for the gift of myself I had
poured out these twenty-nine years.
The Provincial, Sister Rosemary
dispensed me of my vows
that August day. We signed
papers from the Pope, both of us
awkward. Sister Barbara was there
more steady as a witness.

I loved that car: four doors, maroon,
the convent's best, a 1987 Dodge Shadow,
the basic model, no frills, but a key
to freedom. I drive to my apartment,
feeling the grip of these wheels,
four windows wide open.
The wind at my back propels

my parade to Paradise
that is now unfolding.

In Gratitude

I thank all who inspired and coached me in the publishing of this chapbook. Gratitude to Barbara Helfgott Hyett, Grey Held, and the members of the Poetry Round Table: poets who encouraged me to tell this story and helped me find words to express it. Particular thanks to Grey for reading my manuscript and helping me make the final edits. To my lifelong friends who entered the Sisters of Mercy with me: Kathy, Fran, Ellen, Sandy, Beat, and Susan, thanks for your loving laughter about our early lives. To my parents, Bill and Theresa, and my siblings: Maureen, Bill, Ted, Kathy, and Kevin, you are the foundation of my faith and trust in life—and continue to be! Thanks also to Jim Lindsley who was able to hear and encourage my emerging spirit through this lifelong journey.

Sharon A Foley has had poems published in *Nixes Mate Review, Words and Sports, Paterson Literary Review, Euphony, and SWWIM Everyday*. She entered the Sisters of Mercy at age eighteen and lived with them as a nun for twenty-nine years. Ms. Foley has a BA in English from Salve Regina University, and an MSW from Simmons University. For many years she worked as a school social worker. She is now a private practice psychotherapist, and resides in Attleboro, Massachusetts. Her chapbook, *A Kind of Mercy*, was named as a finalist in the Lefty Blondie Press First Chapbook Award.

www.ingramcontent.com/pod-product-compliance
Lightning Source LLC
Chambersburg PA
CBHW020223090426
42734CB00008B/1189